Juan Serrano

King of the Flamenco Guitar

Solos from Juan Serrano's videos
Juan Serrano/Flamenco Guitar and *Juan Serrano/The Flamenco Tradition, Part 1*

Online Audio   www.melbay.com/96328BCDEB

AUDIO CONTENTS

1 Farrucas (2:45)	**7** Lamento Gitano (5:29)
2 Soleares (2:02)	**8** La Juderia (4:56)
3 Lagriamas de Granda (6:19)	**9** Cueva Gitana (6:44)
4 Nostalgia (3:43)	**10** Punta Umbria (4:43)
5 Fantasy (6:47)	**11** Tarifa (4:41)
6 Dos Colores (5:01)	**12** Amigo Mariano (4:09)

---

1 2 3 4 5 6 7 8 9 0

CONTENTS

Juan Serrano
Flamenco Guitar

Flamenco Tradition
The Four Basic Flamenco Songs*

BASIC TECHNIQUES

Rasgueado
No. 1

Juan Serrano

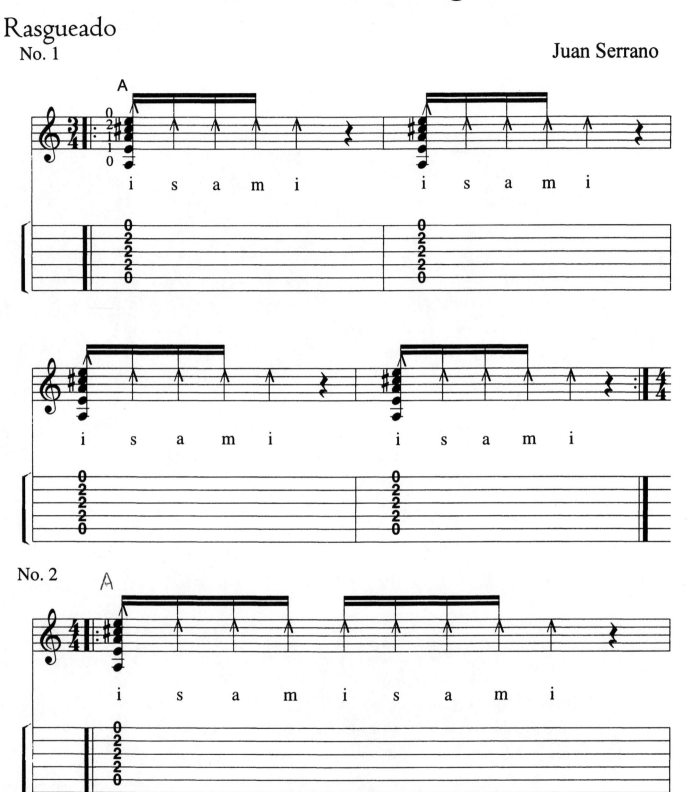

No. 2

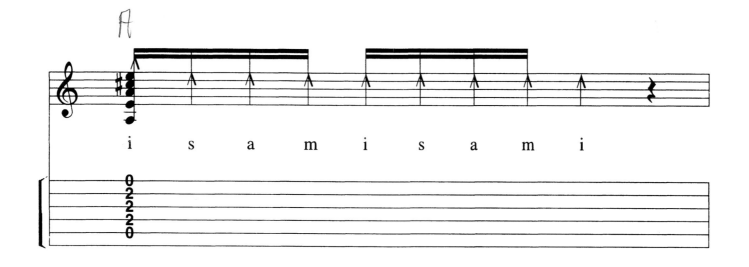

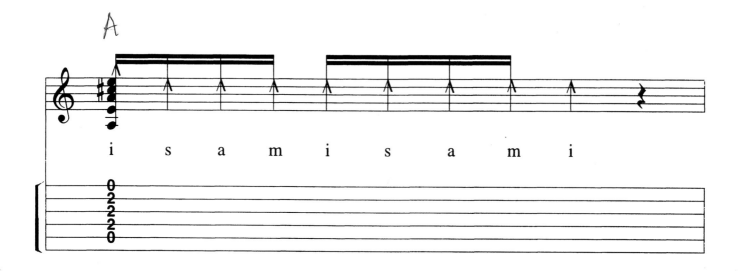

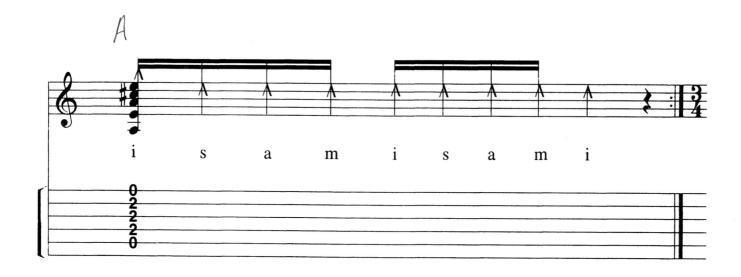

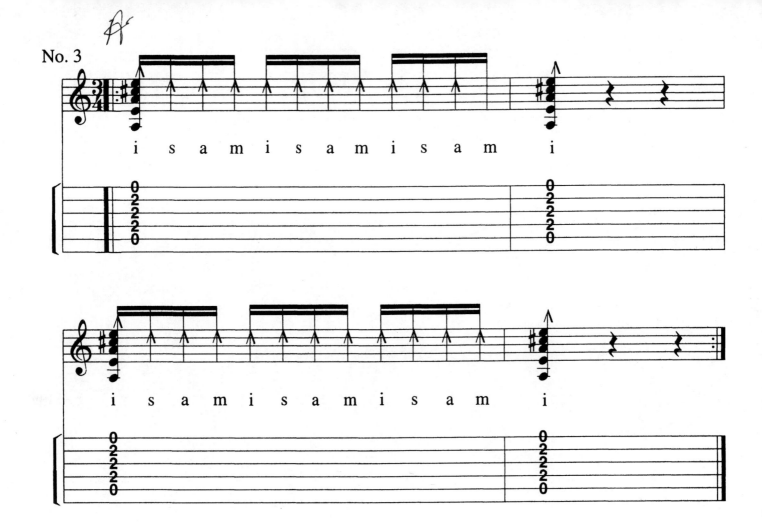

Tremolo Study
No. 1

Juan Serrano

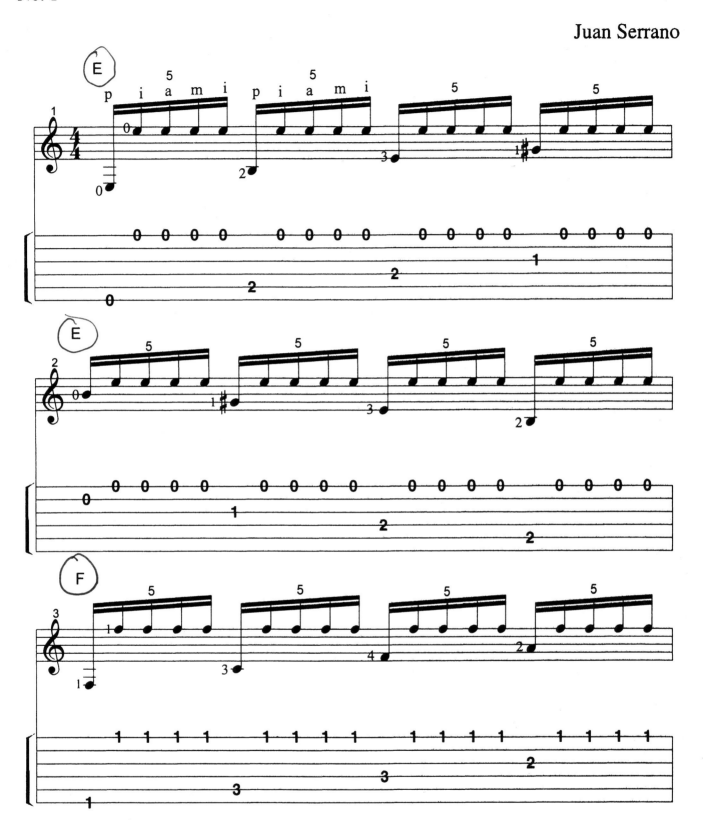

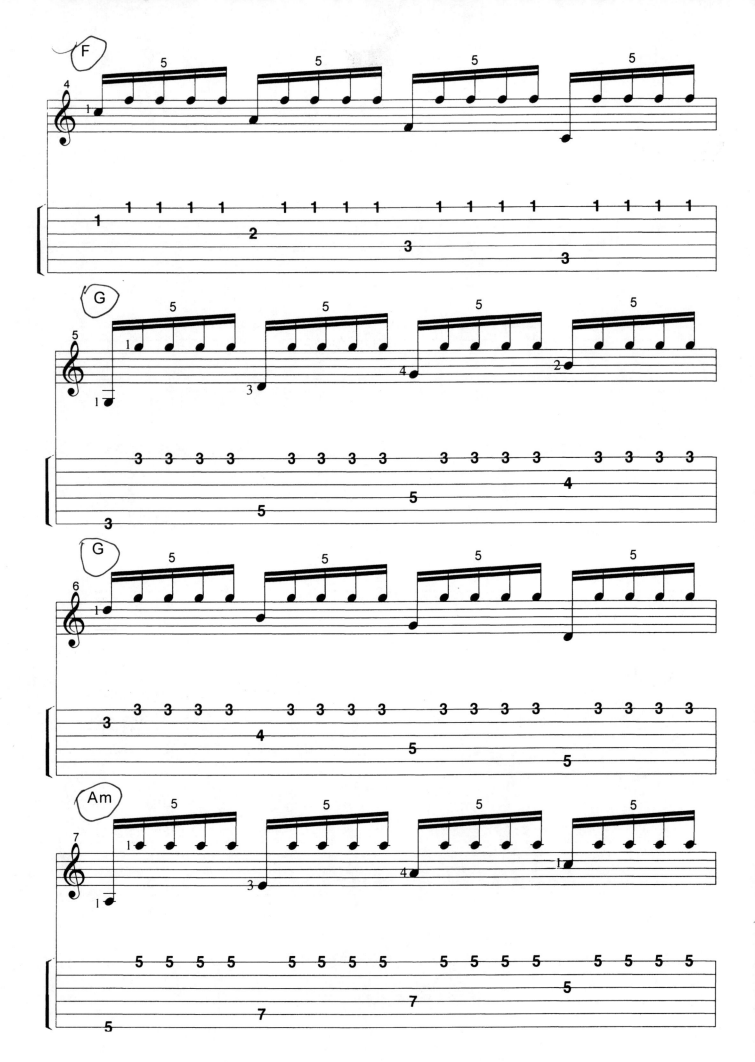

8

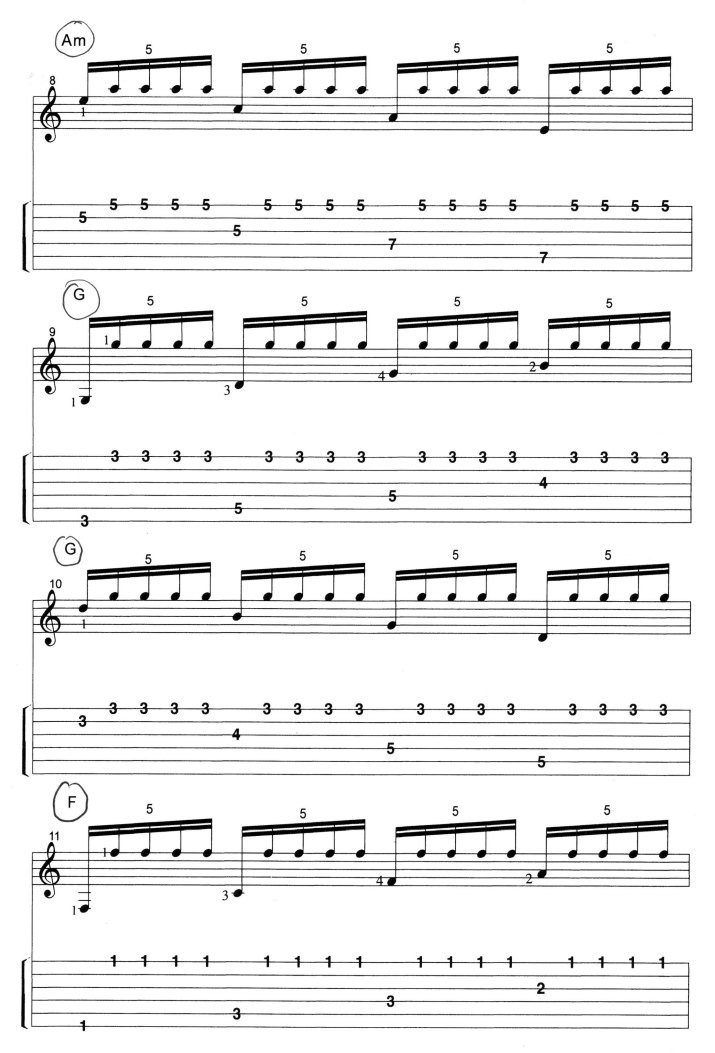

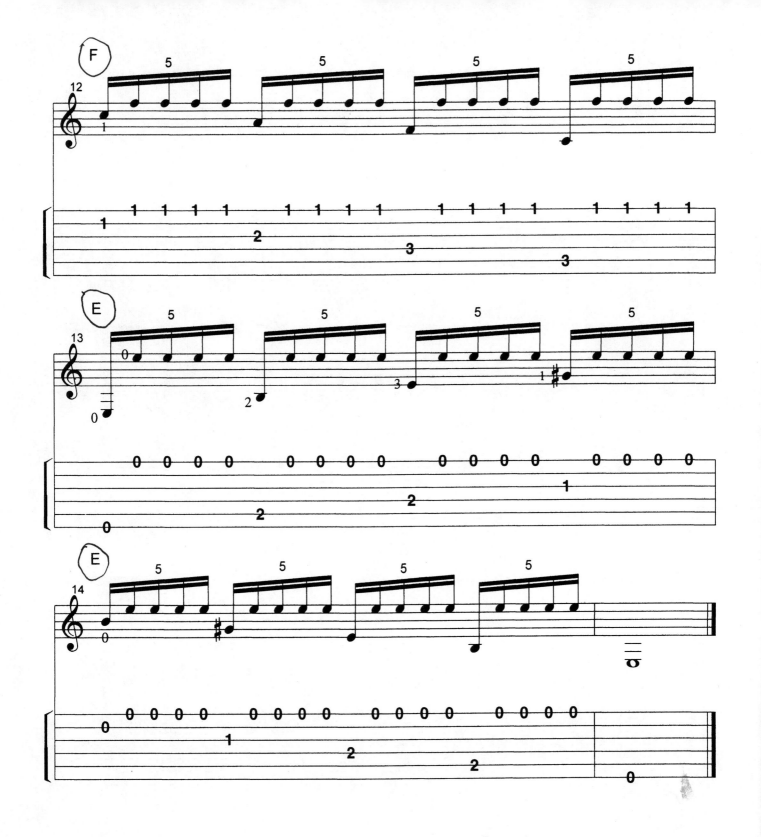

No. 2

Juan Serrano

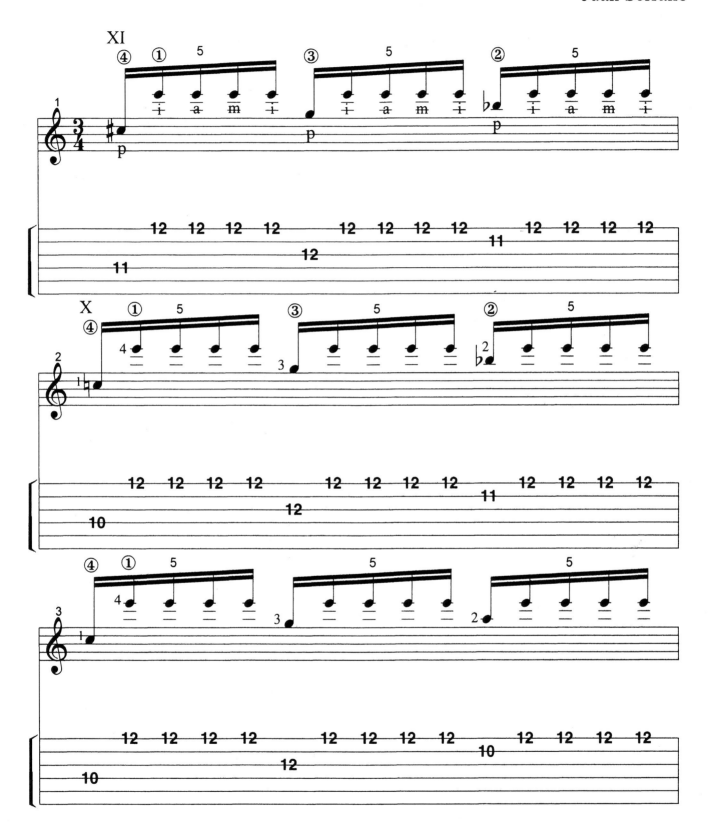

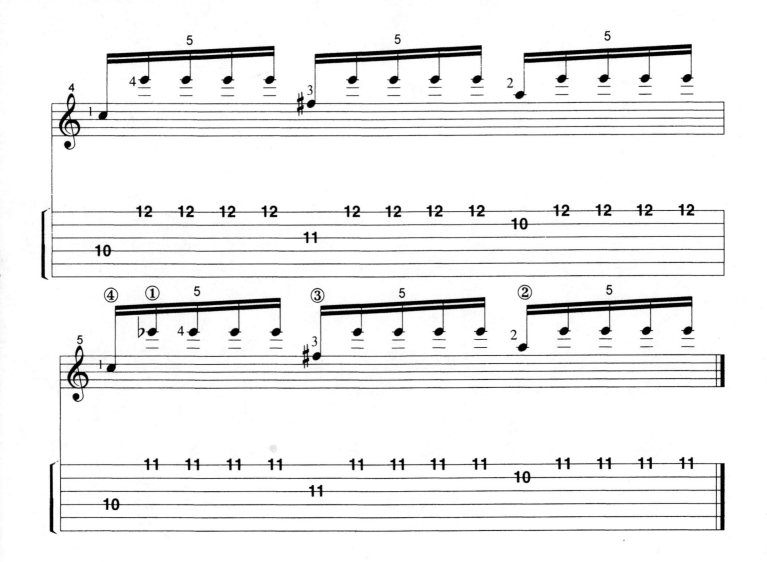

Continue this tremolo study in the same
descending fashion, all the way down the
first position.

Arpeggio Exercise
No. 1

Juan Serrano

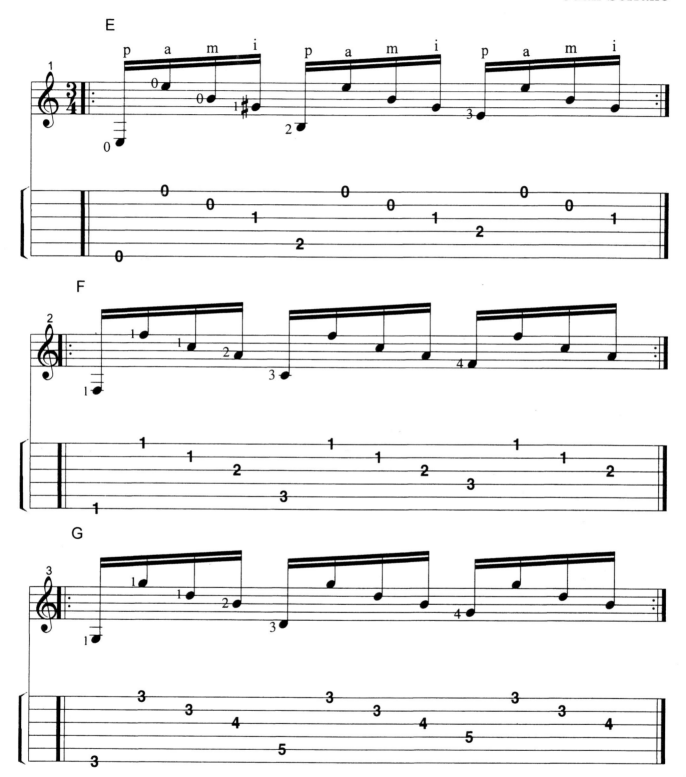

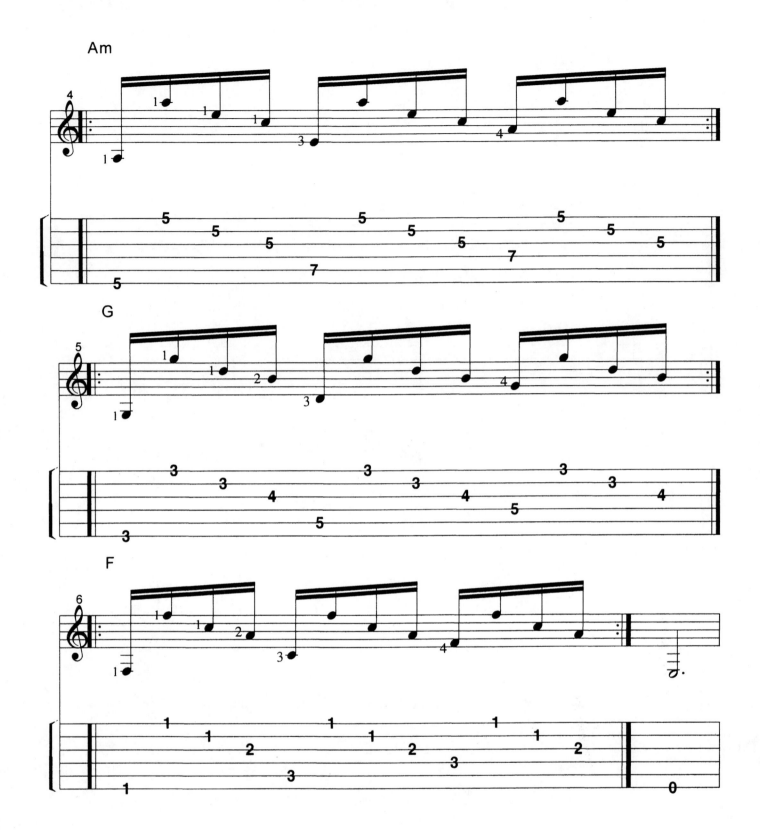

No. 2

Repeat for chords F-G-Am-G-F
(same as exer. No. 1)

No. 3

Repeat for chords F-G-Am-G-F

No. 4

Repeat for chords F-G-Am-G-F

Picado
No. 1

Juan Serrano

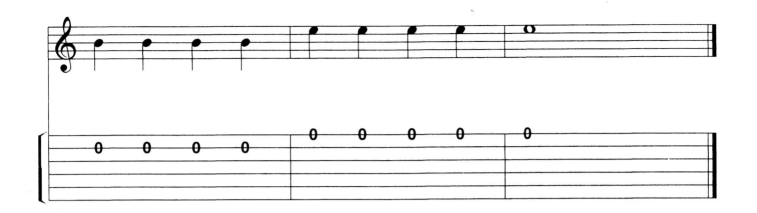

No. 2

Juan Serrano

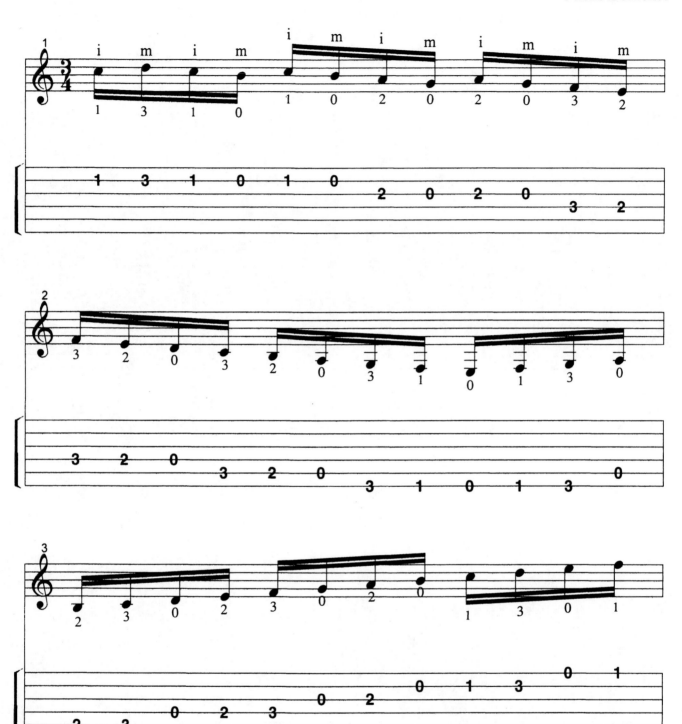

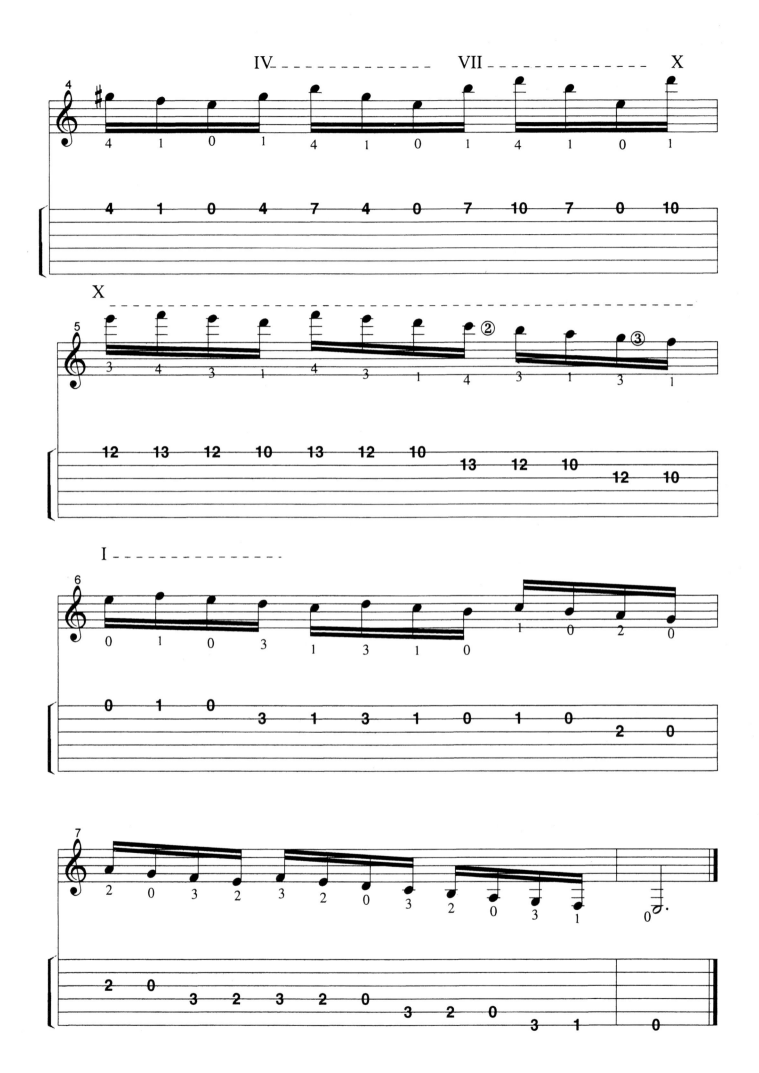

Golpe

No. 1

G SYMBOL FOR THE SPANISH WORD "GOLPE"---MEANING TO TAP THE TOP OF THE GUITAR ONLY WITH THE ANULAR (a) FINGER TIP.

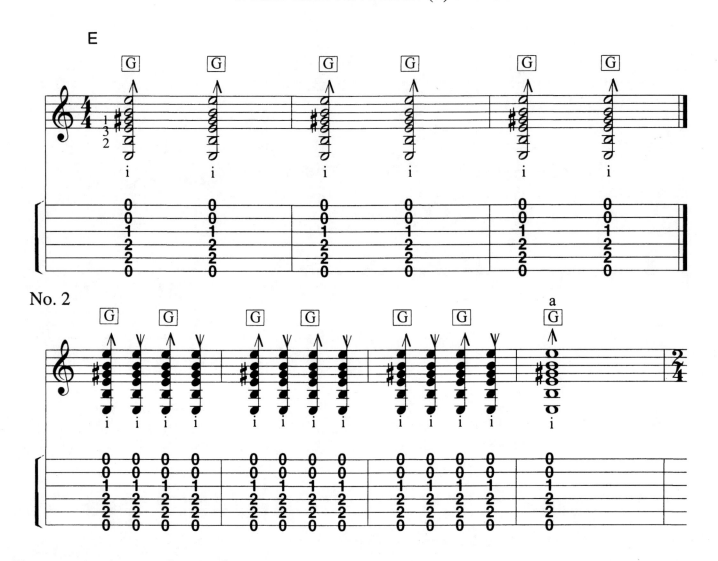

No. 2

Rasgueado with Golpe

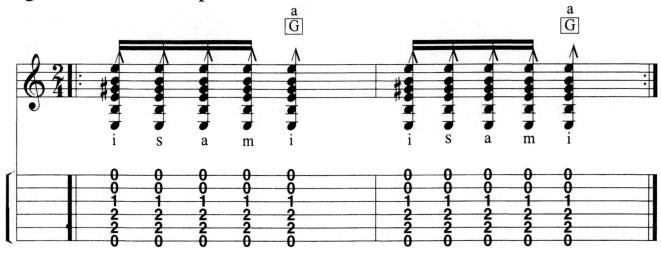

20

Farrucas

Juan Serrano

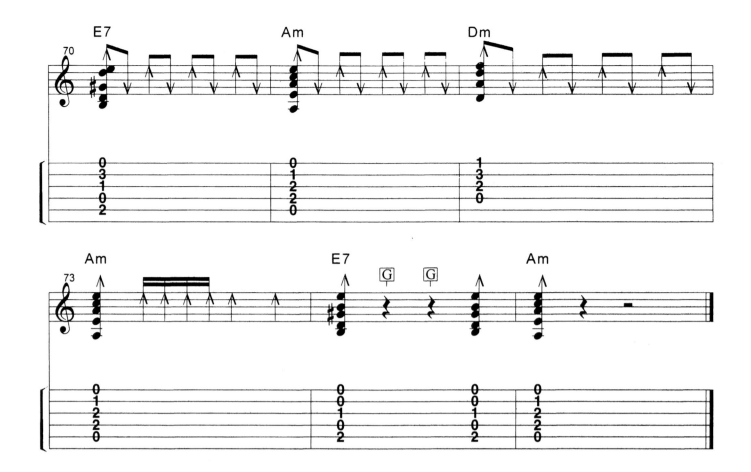

Soleares

Juan Serrano

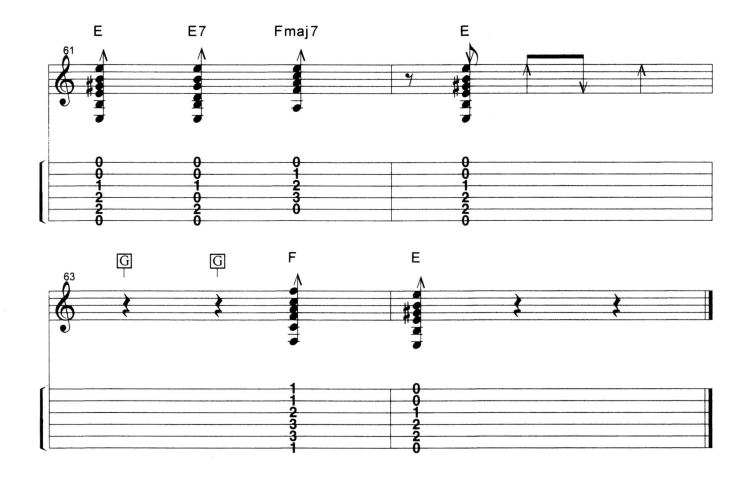

33

LAGRIAMAS DE GRANDA

(Granainas)

In this selection you will hear the feel of the Arabic/Spanish influence in flamenco. For 800 years, regions of southern Spain were ruled by the Moors from North Africa, until they were driven out by the campaigns of Isabel and Ferdinand in 1492. This composition, "Lagrimas de Granada," was inspired by the last Arabic king who abandoned the city of Granada because it could not be saved from takeover by Christian armies. Legend says that while fleeing to the outskirts of the city, the King, Abu 'Abd Allah – known in Spain as Boabdil "el chico" – wept while being admonished by his old nursemaid: "You cry like a child for what you could not defend as a man."

This emotional piece is a Granainas.

Juan Serrano

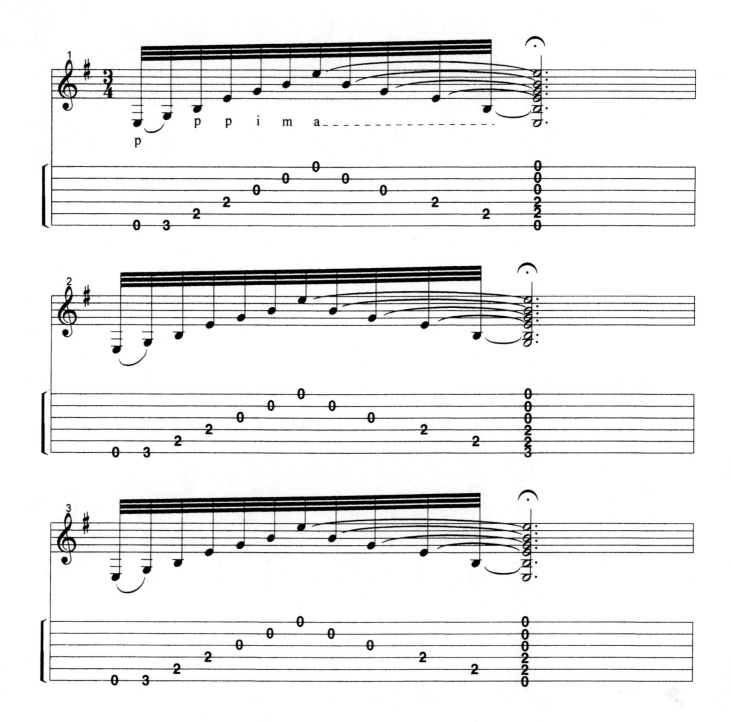

34

CIII

38

39

41

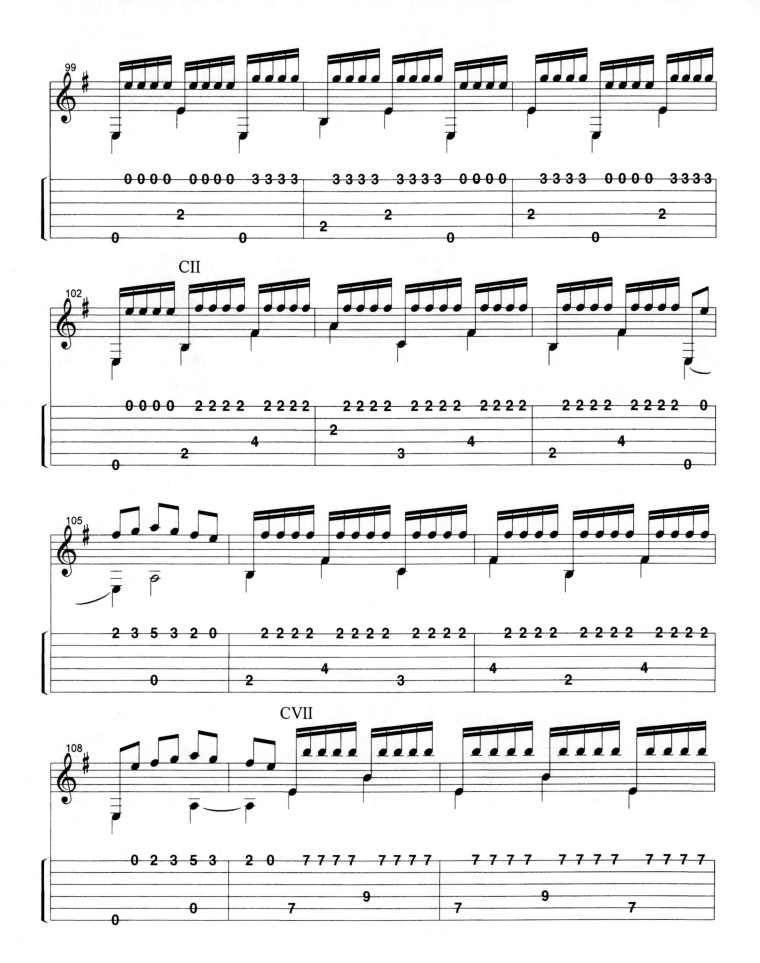

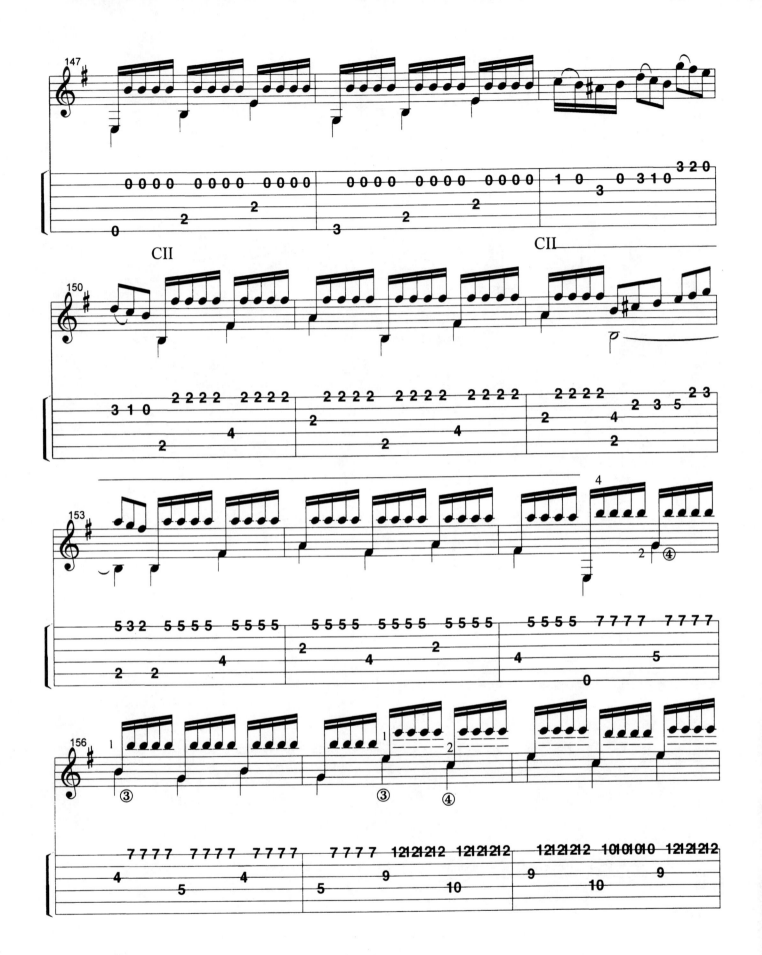

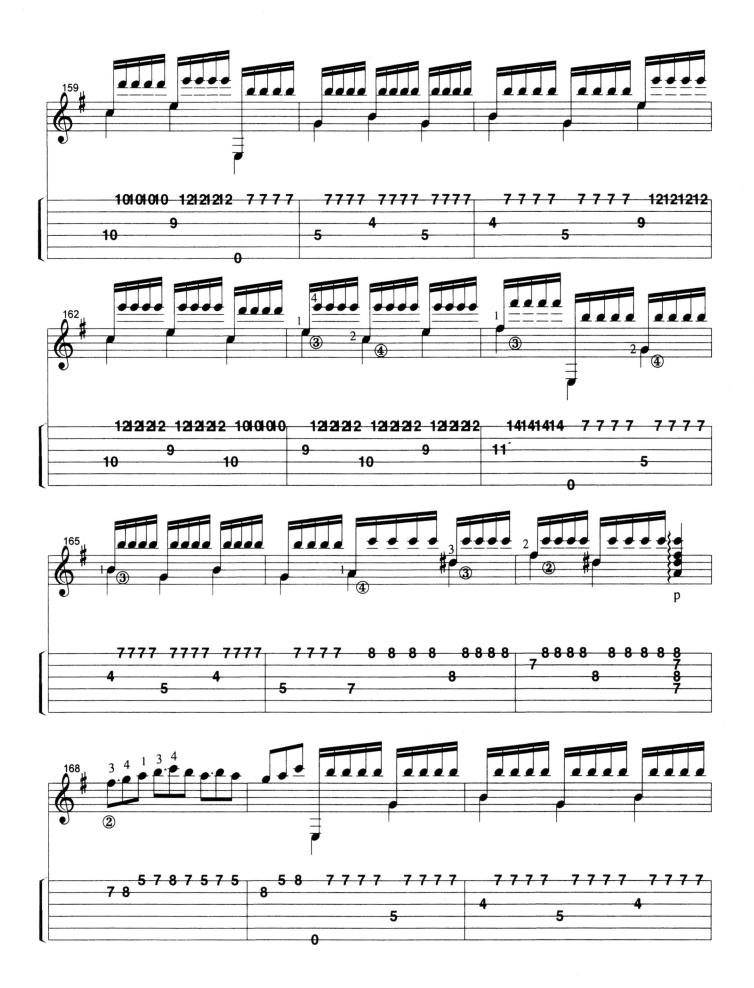

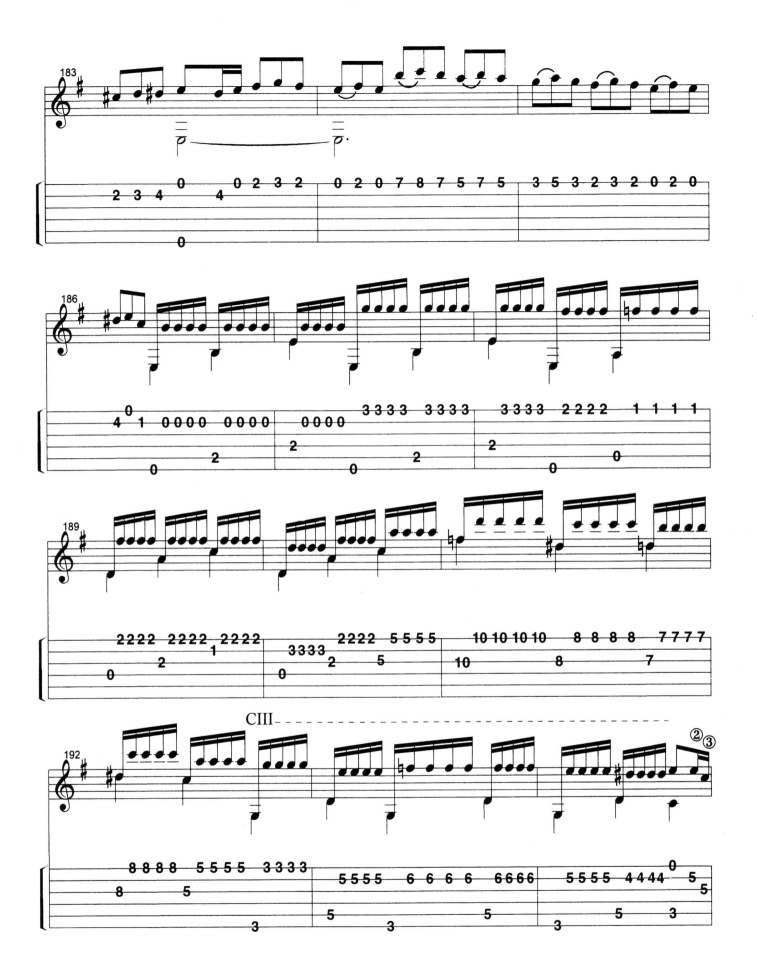

54

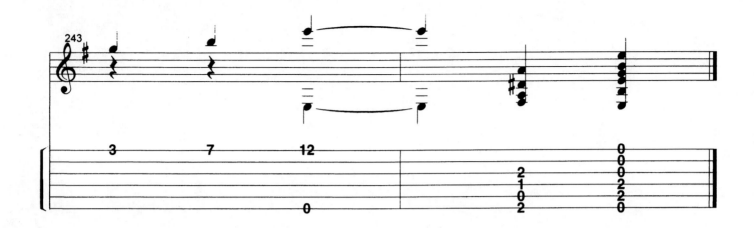

NOSTALGIA
(Guajiras)

Juan Serrano

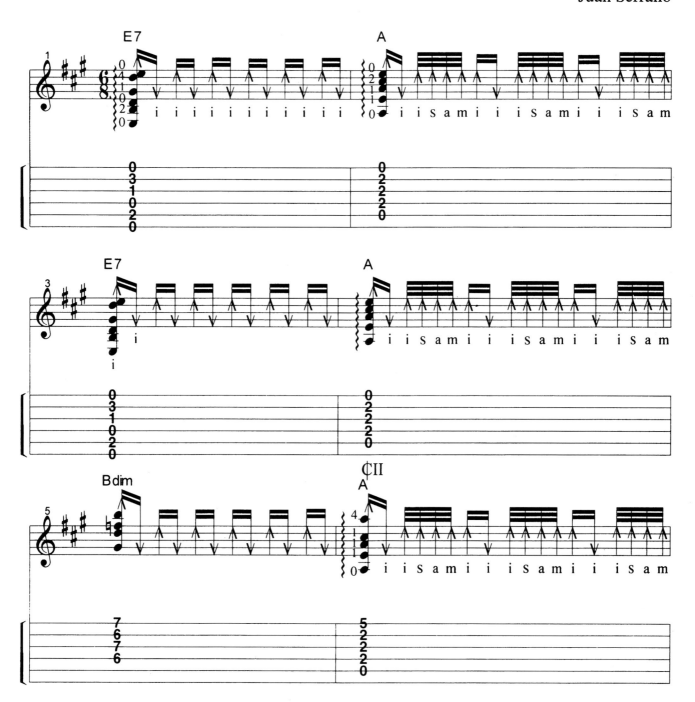

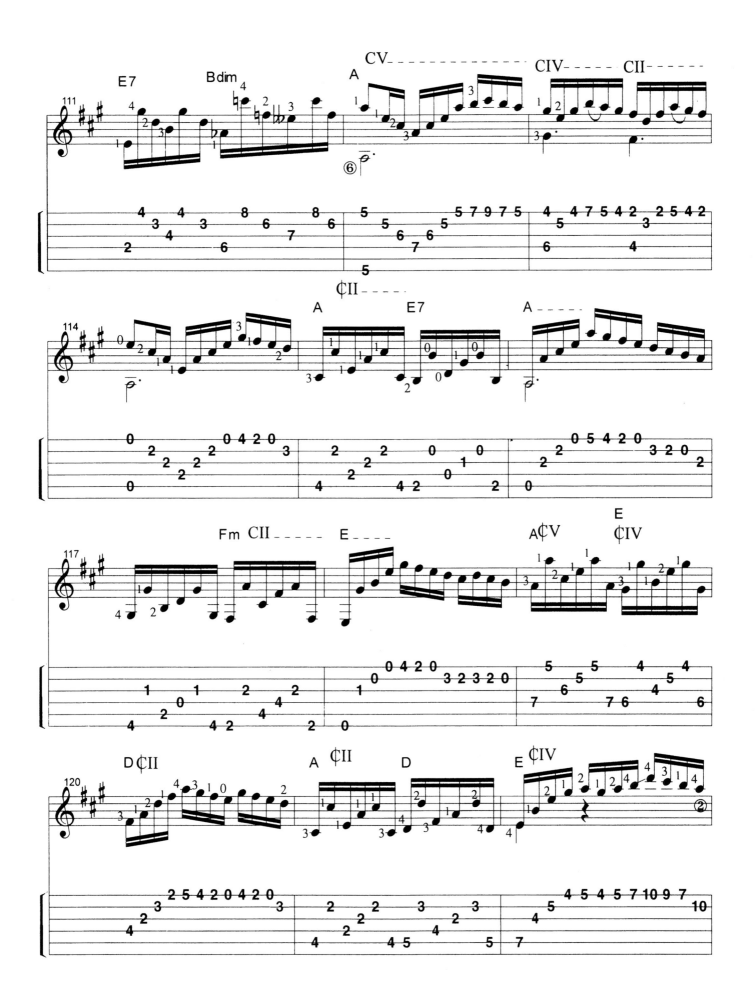

FANTASY
(Zambra)

6TH=D (Re)

Juan Serrano

DOS COLORES

(Solea por Bulerias)

Juan Serrano

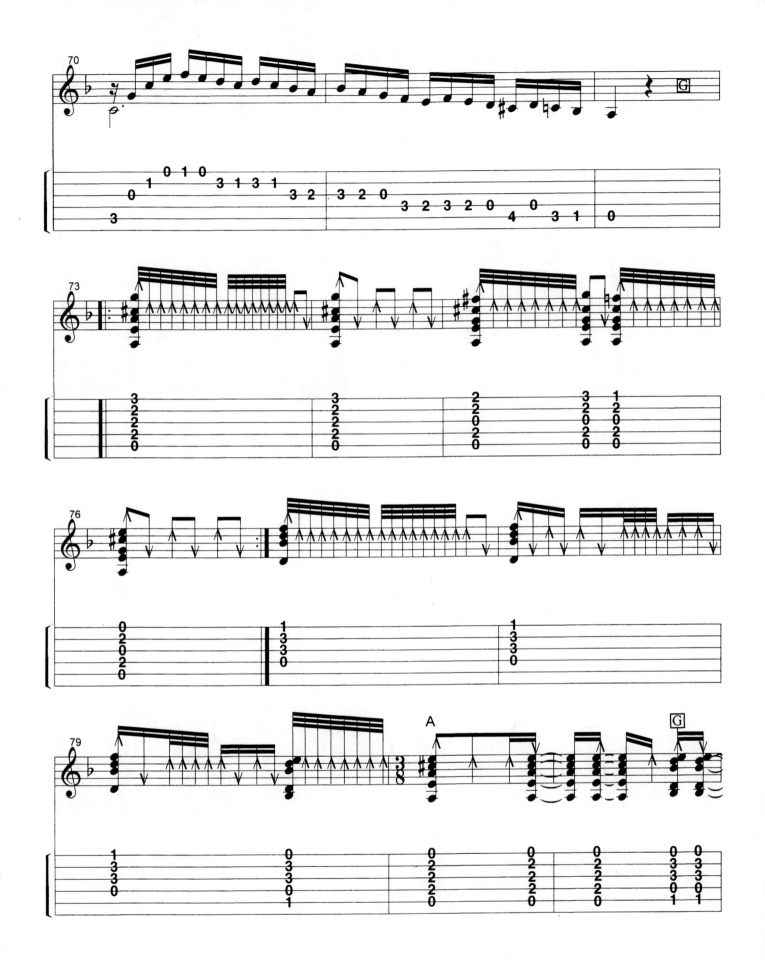

99

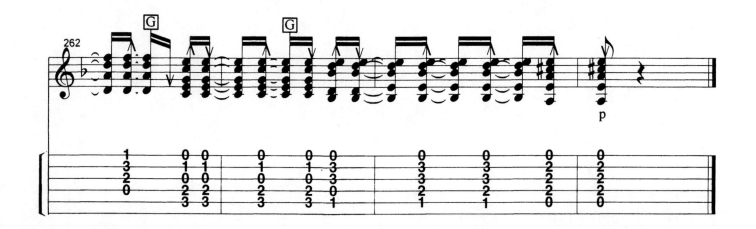

FLAMENCO TRADITION

The substance of the *cante flamenco* is a mosaic of Greek, Hindu, Hebrew, Arabic, pagan and Oriental cultures and musical forms which contributed to the making of Andalusian folklore. The *toná*, the matrix of all *flamenco cantes*, sprang from the grafting of the gypsy soul into this Andalusian folklore. It constitutes the purest and most venerable starting point of flamenco, that is the oldest manifestation of the gypsy–Andalusian art form that we know. The *toná* was a song without guitar accompaniment.

The gypsy nomads, living at the fringes of society, persecuted and imprisoned, crystallized their sorrows not only in *tonás* but also in *siguiriyas*, *soleares*, *tangos* and *fandangos*. If the *toná* is the matrix of the *cante*, the *siguiriya*, *soleares*, *tangos* and *fandangos* are its basic, "purest" forms. Throughout flamenco's history these forms gave birth to numerous variations based on rhythm, lyrics, or a *tocaor's* interpretation.

The next section of this book contains the four basic forms of flamenco and two of their numerous variations that have inspired profound and creative forms of art.

Dr. José Elgorriaga

LAMENTO GITANO
(Siguiriyas)

Juan Serrano

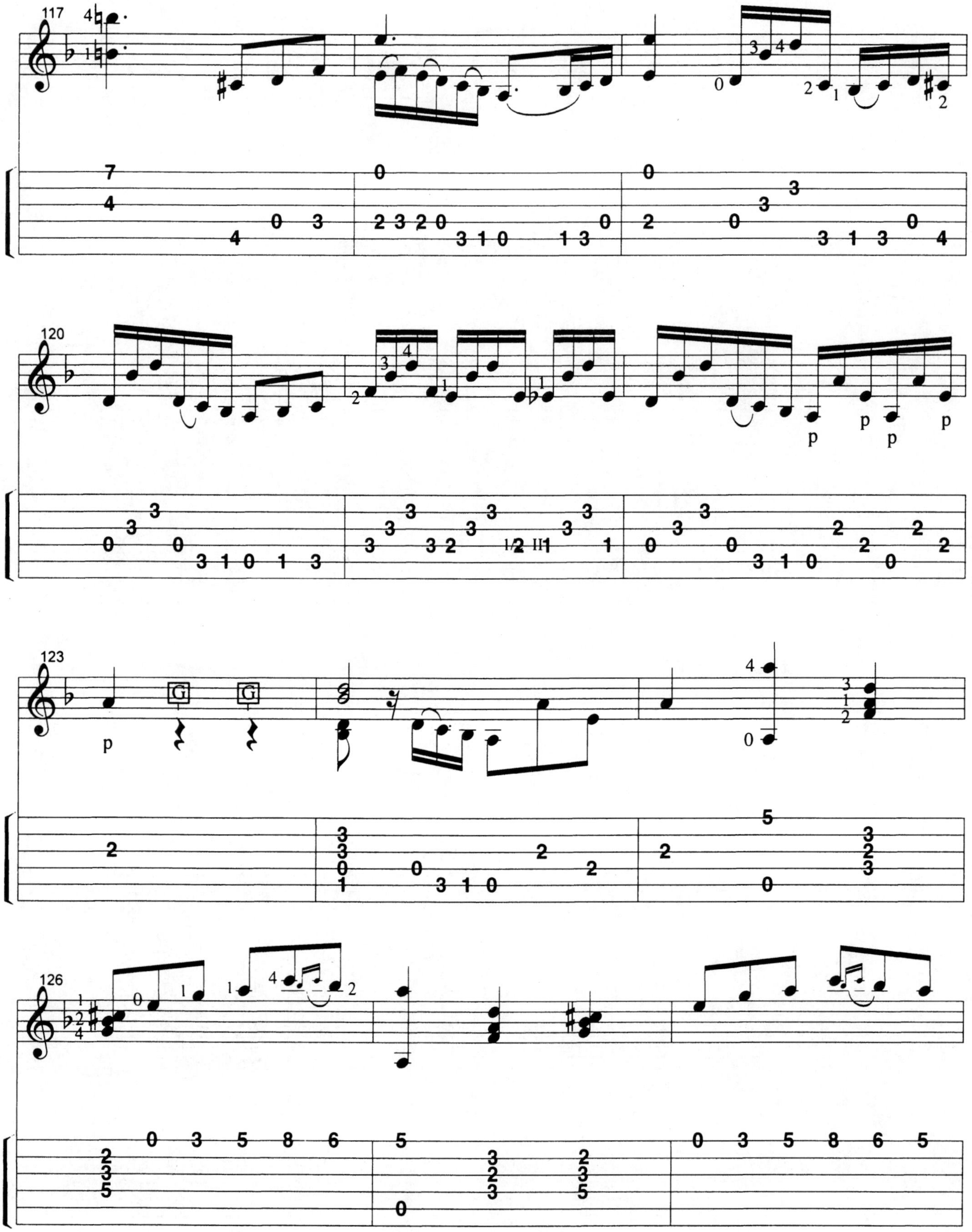
117
120
123
126

TECHNIQUES

Rasgueado

No. 1

Juan Serrano

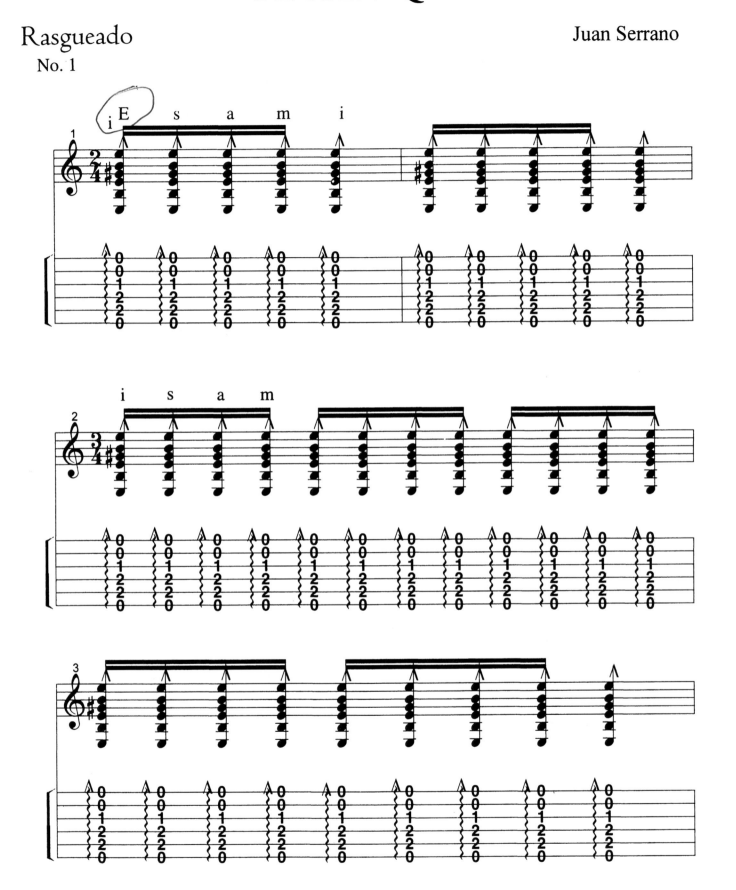

No. 2

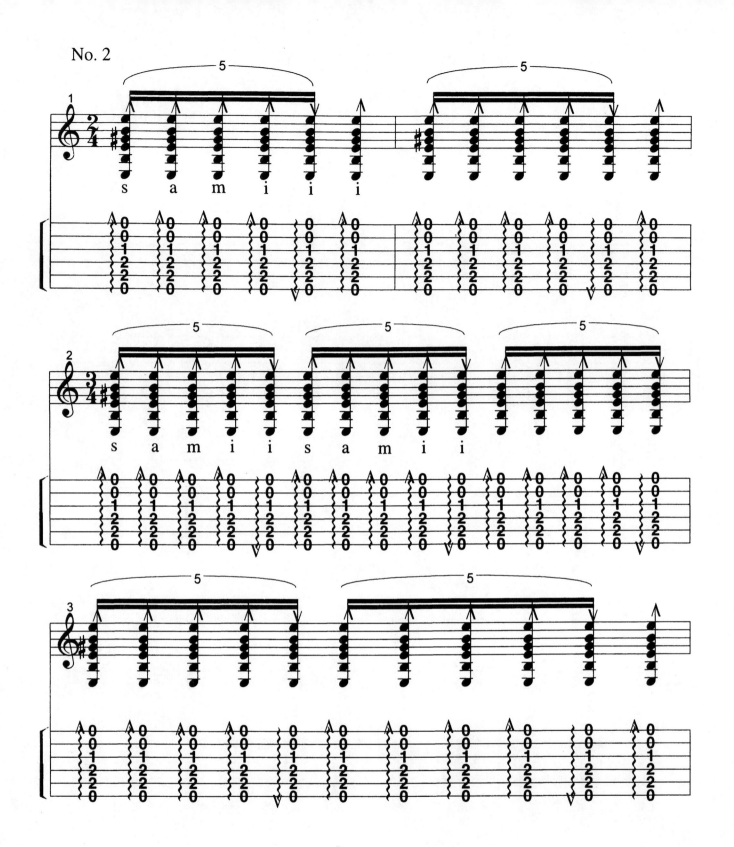

No. 3

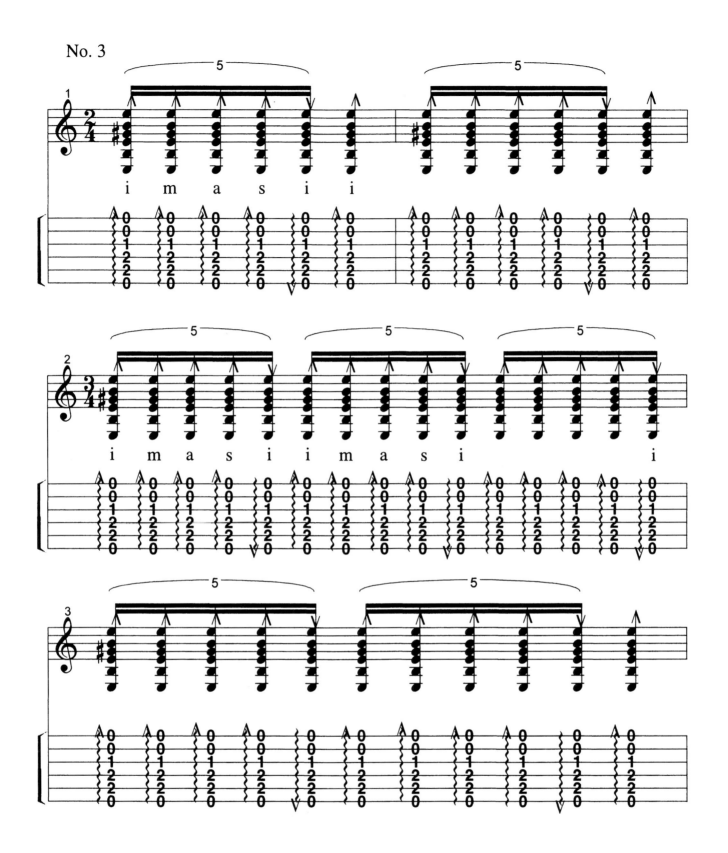

Rasgueado en Abanico

Juan Serrano

No. 1

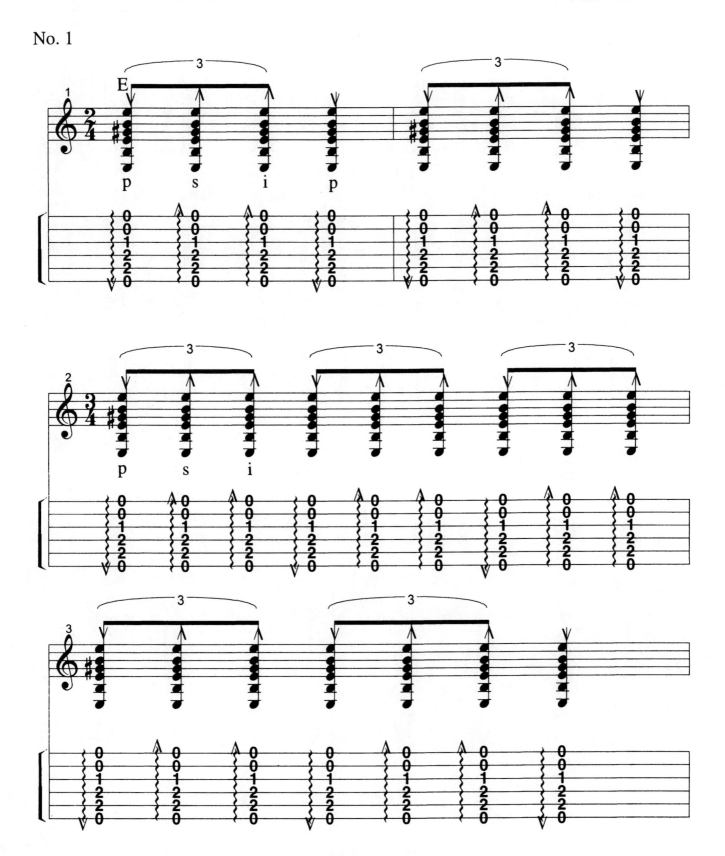

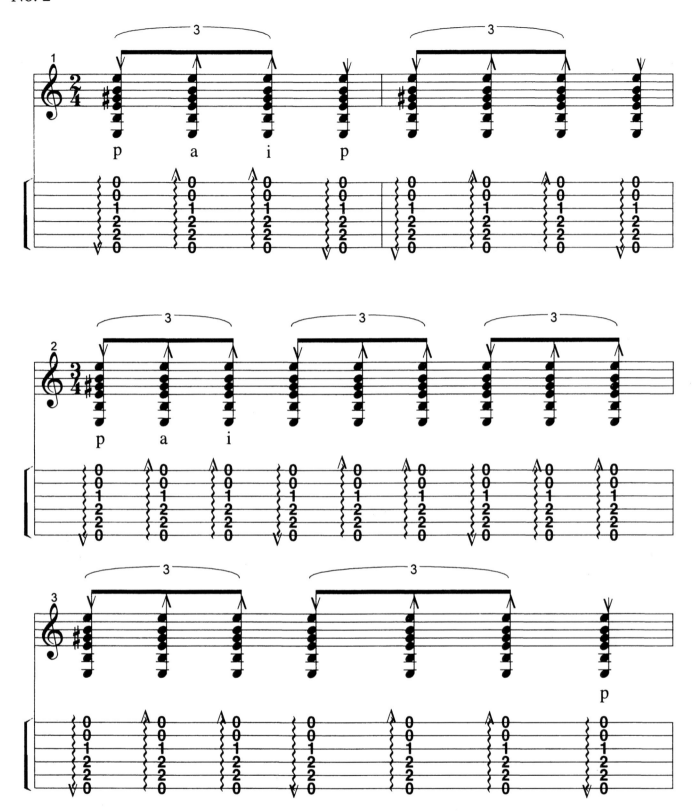

No. 3

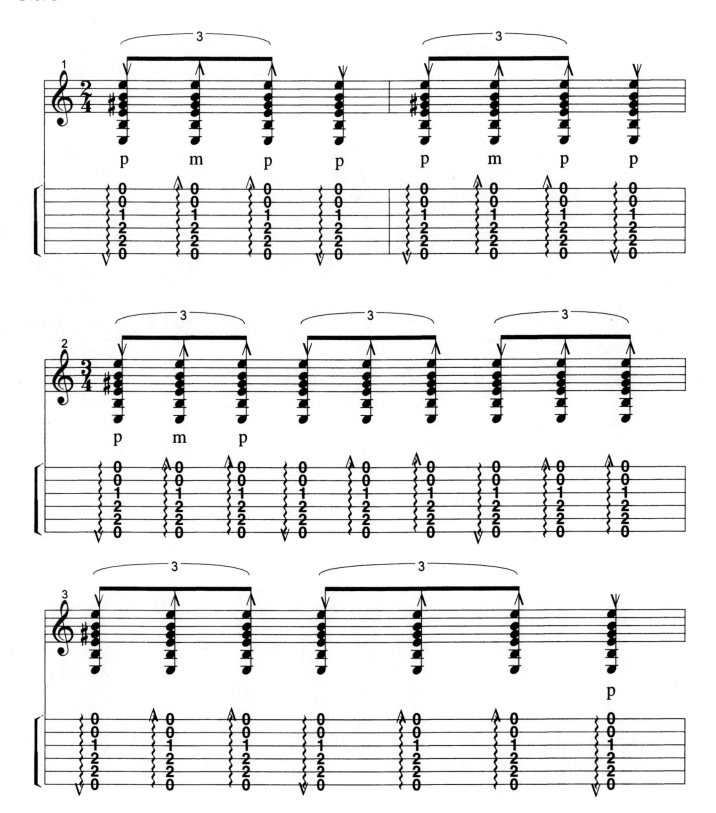

No. 4

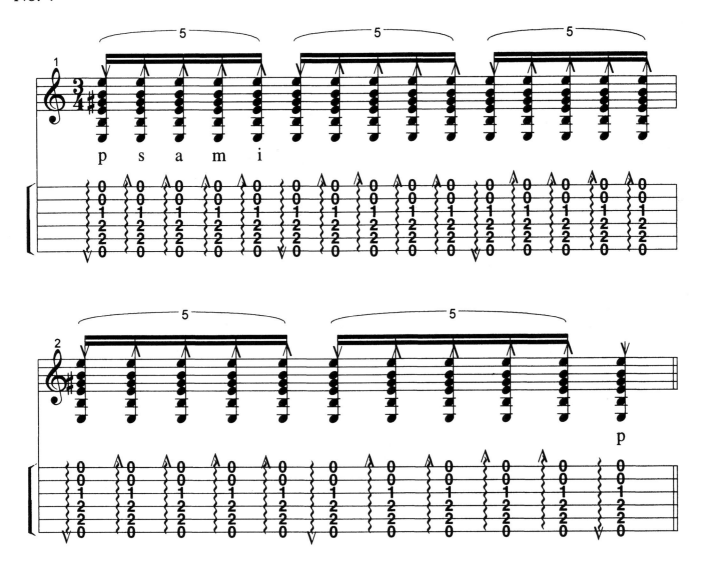

Tremolo

Flamenco

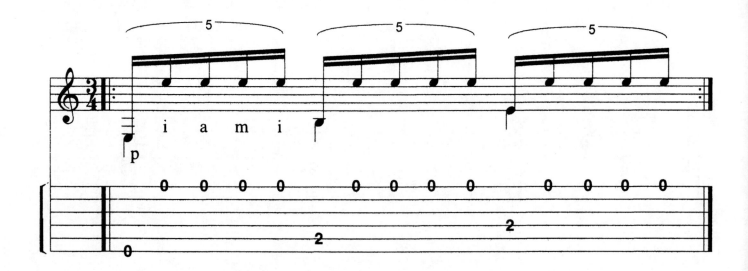

Classical

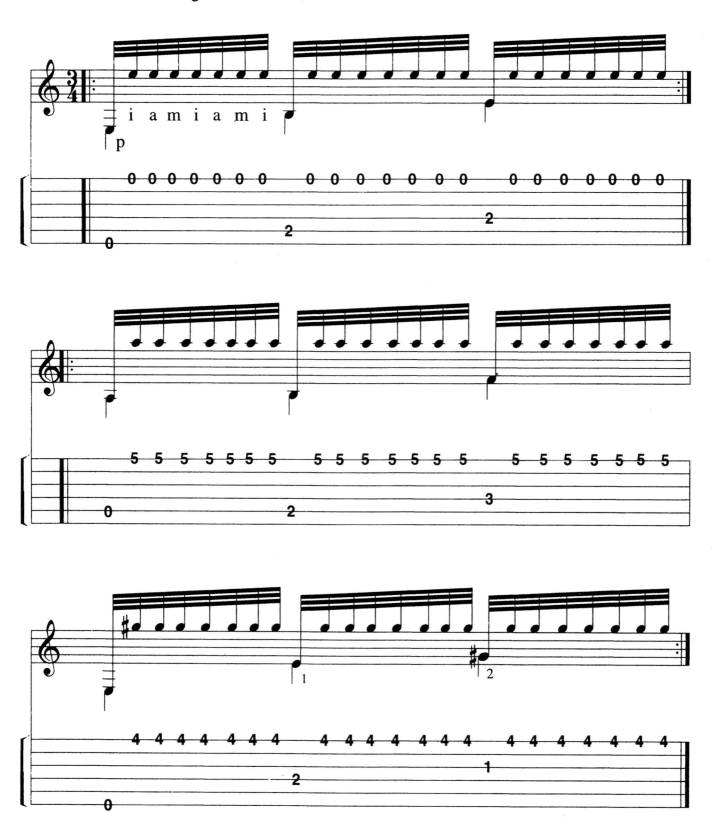

Alzapua

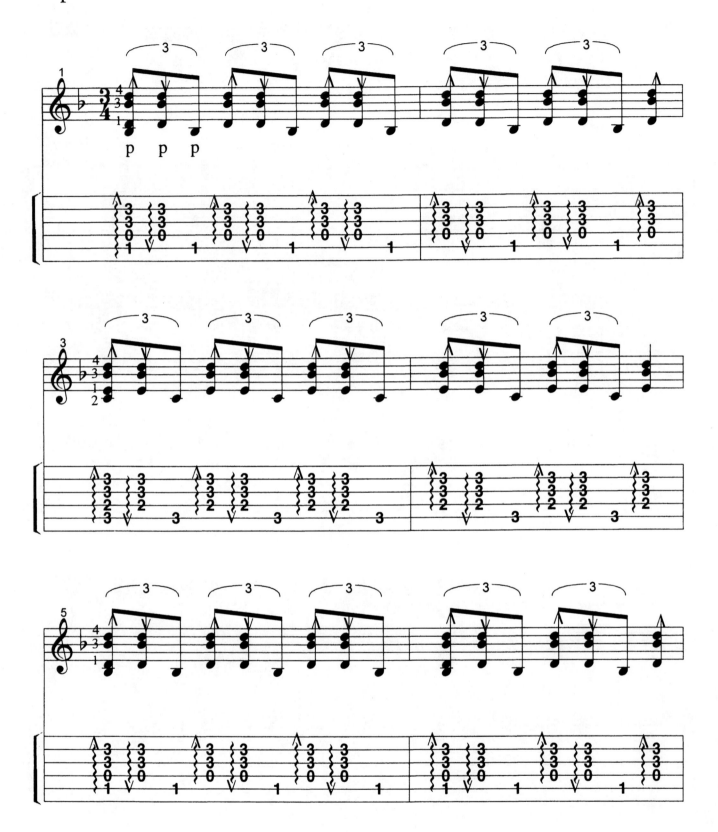

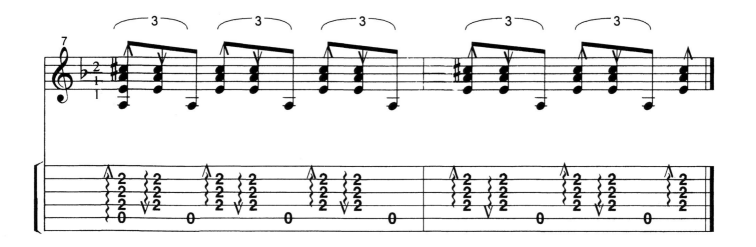

Bulerias Falseta

134

Bulerias Falseta with Alzapua

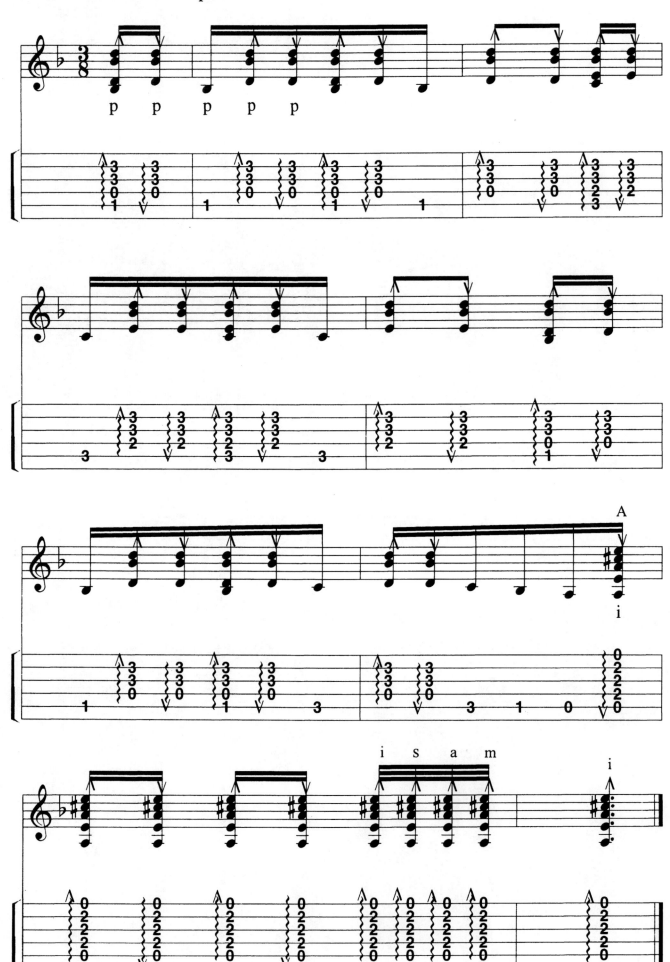

LA JUDERÍA

(Soleares)

Juan Serrano

137

138

143

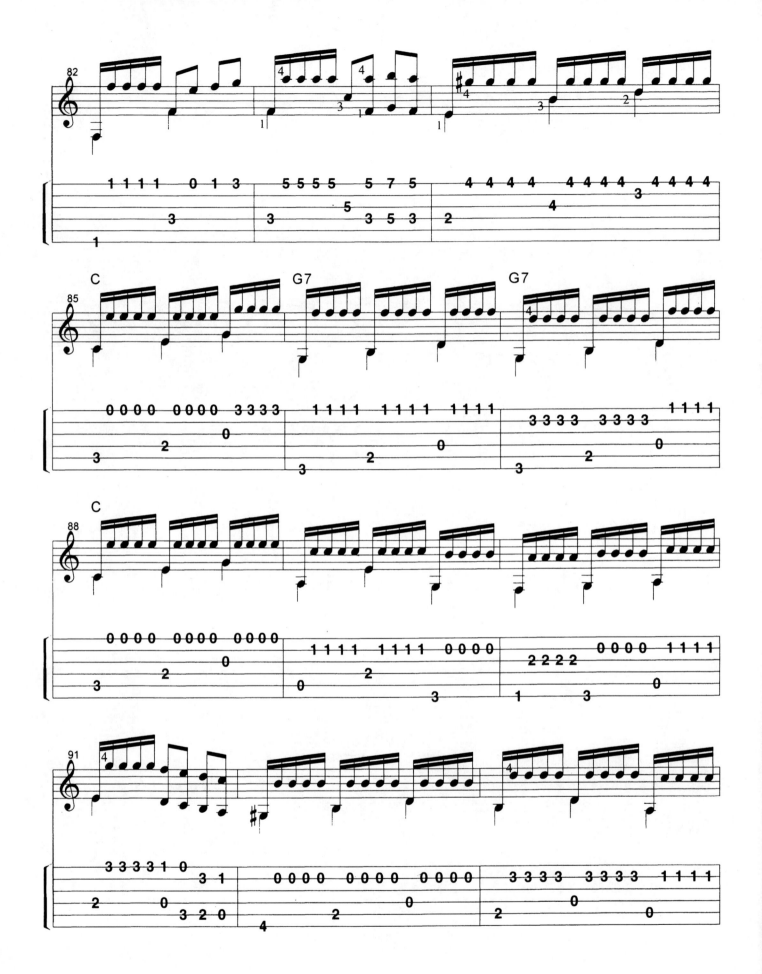

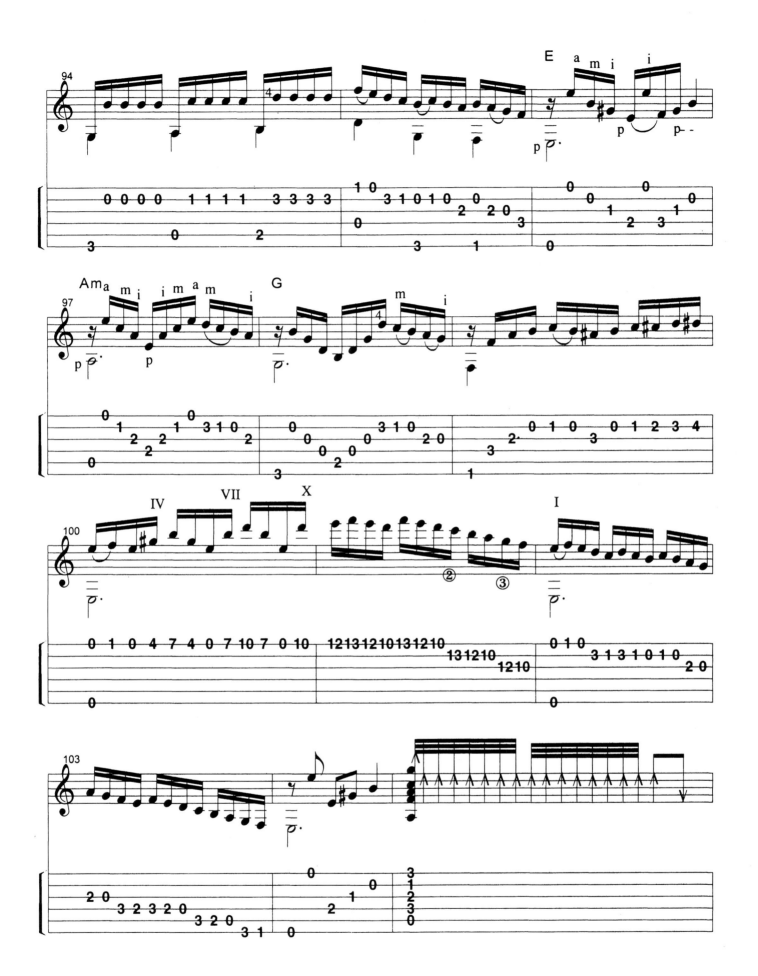

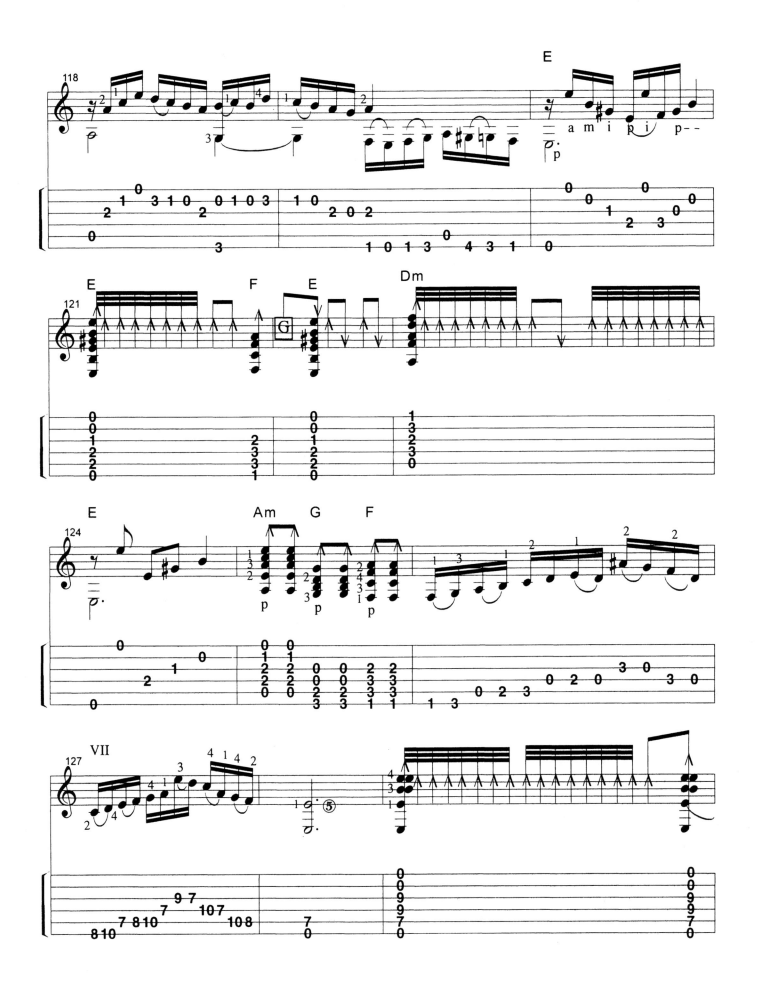

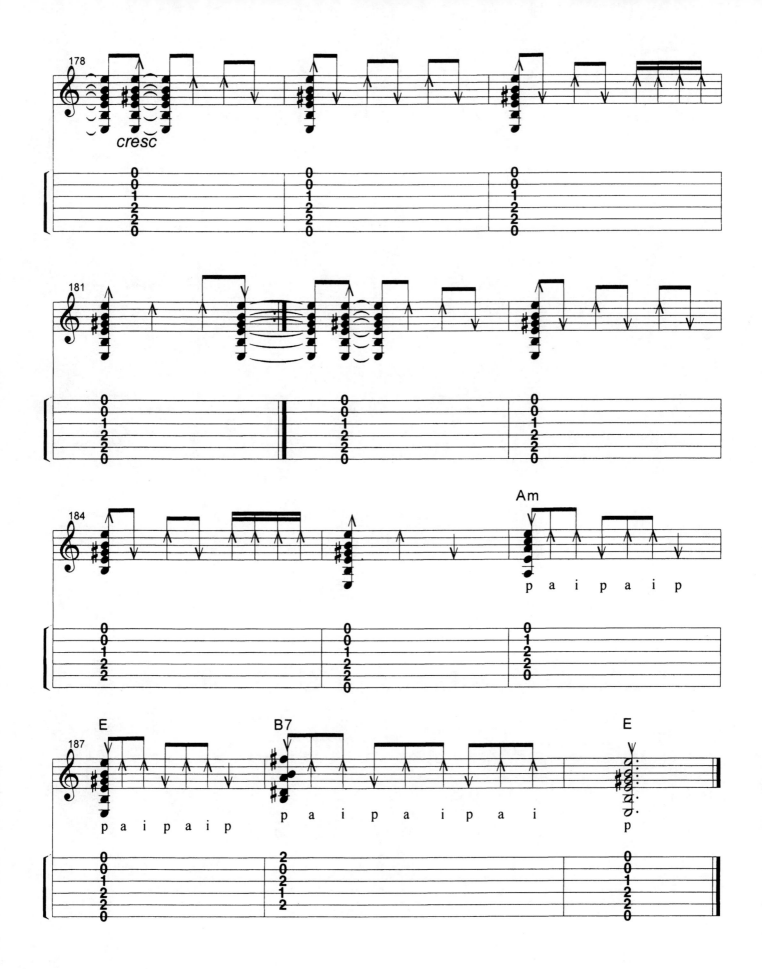

CUEVA GITANA

(Tangos)

Juan Serrano

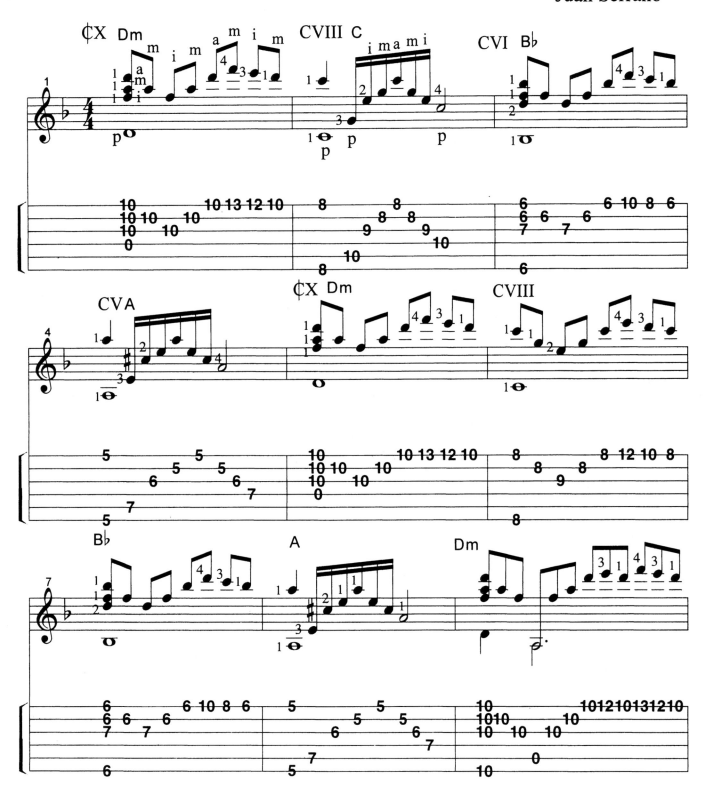

154

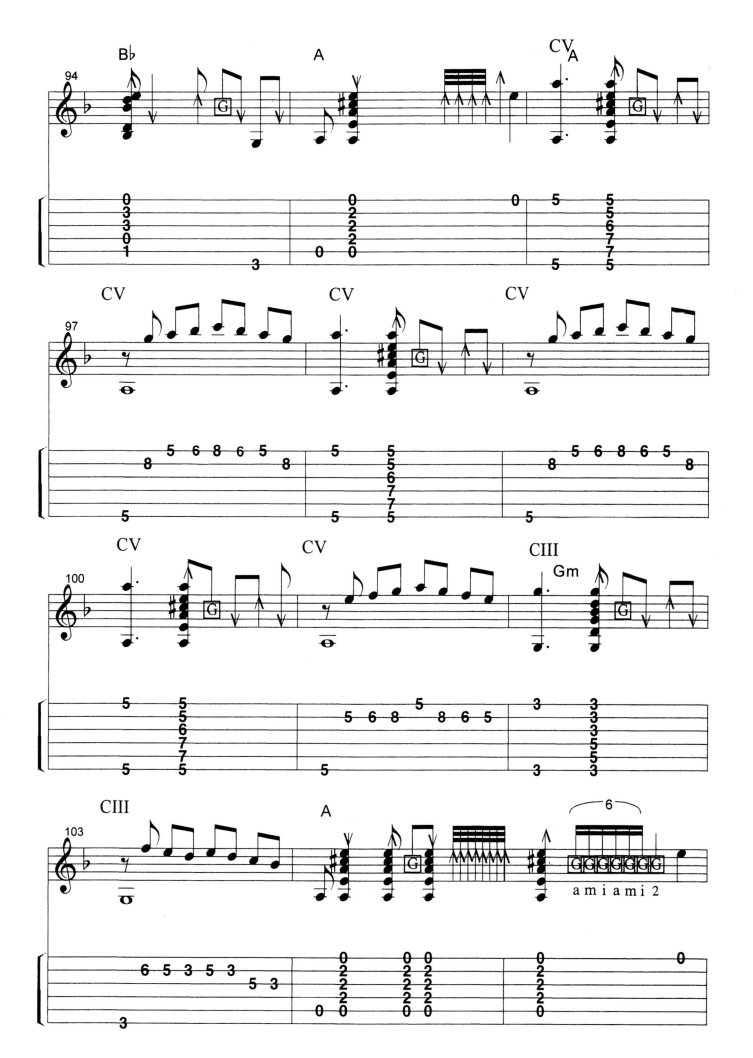

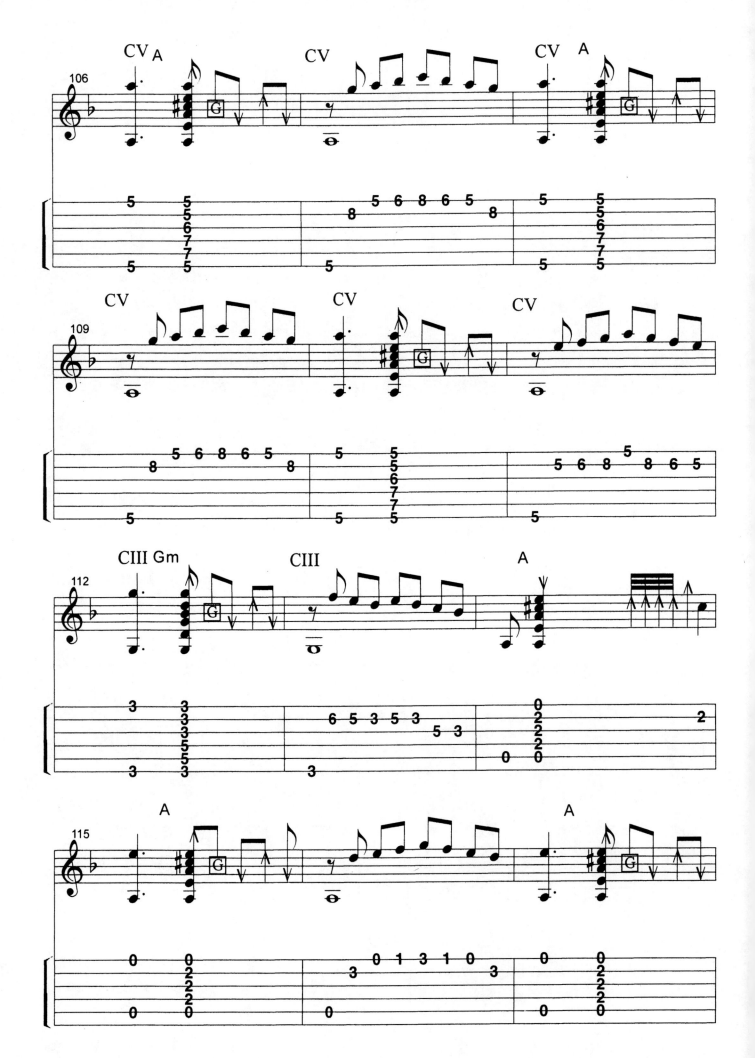

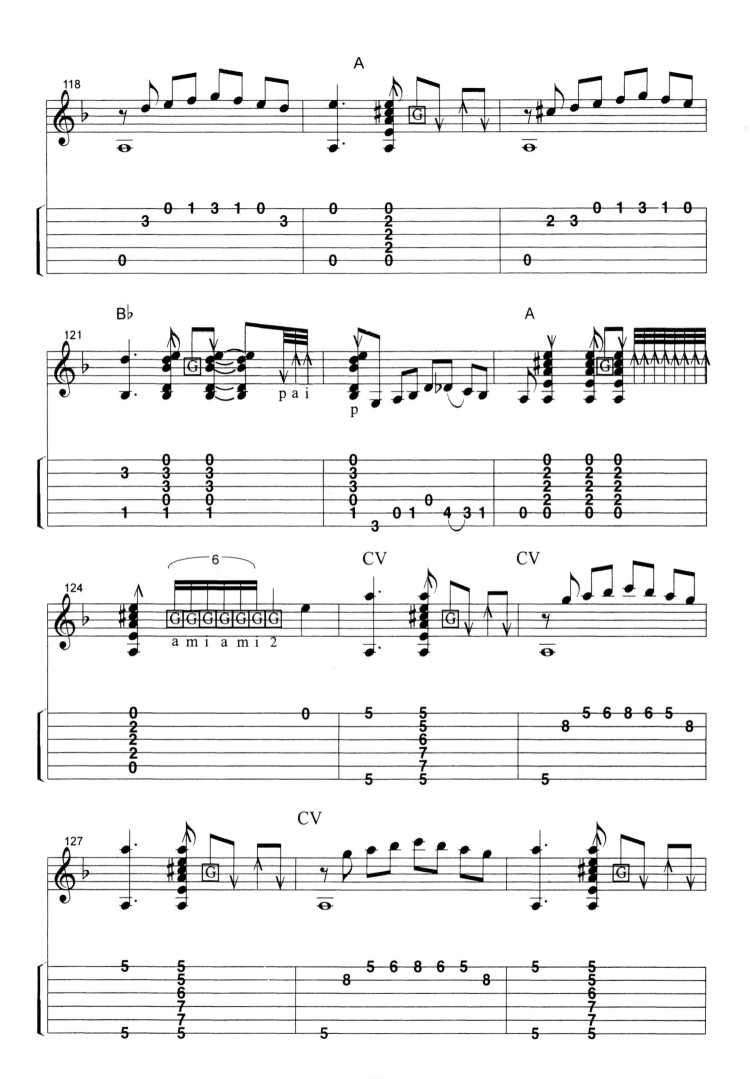

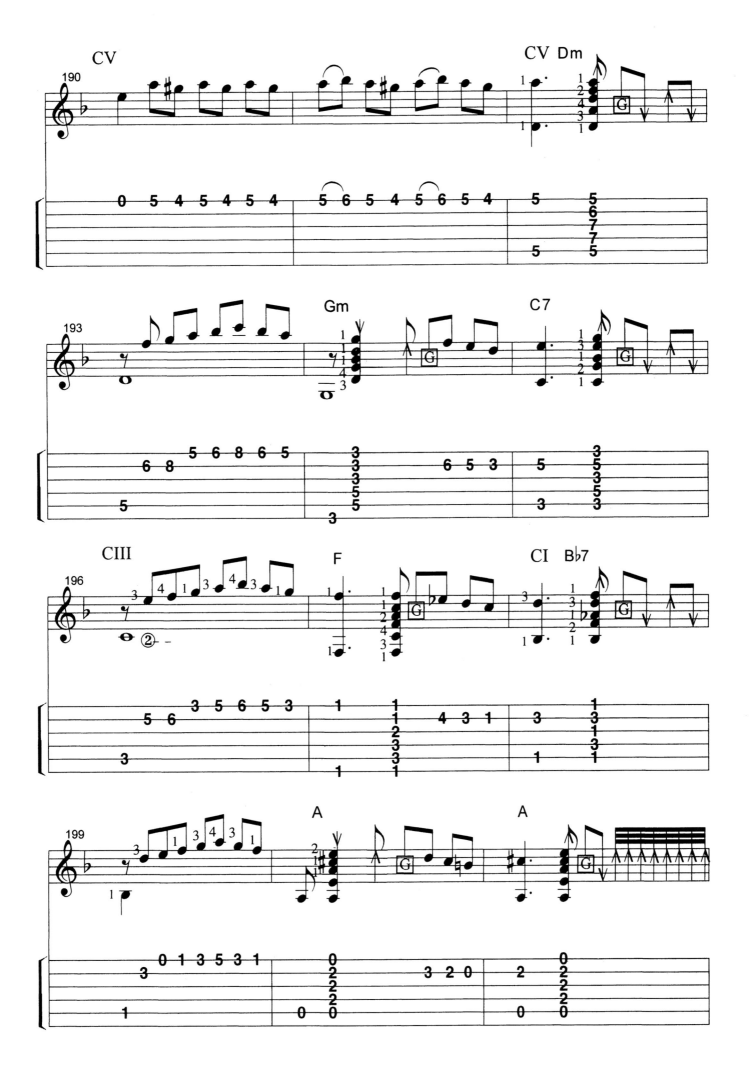

172

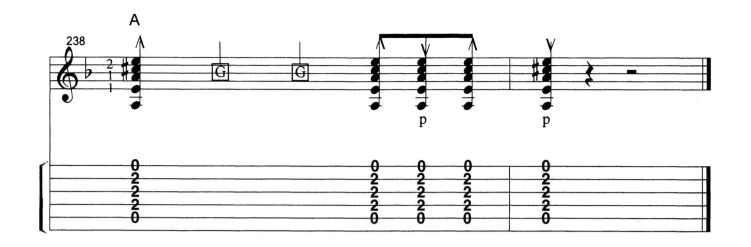

PUNTA UMBRIA

(Fandangos)

Juan Serrano

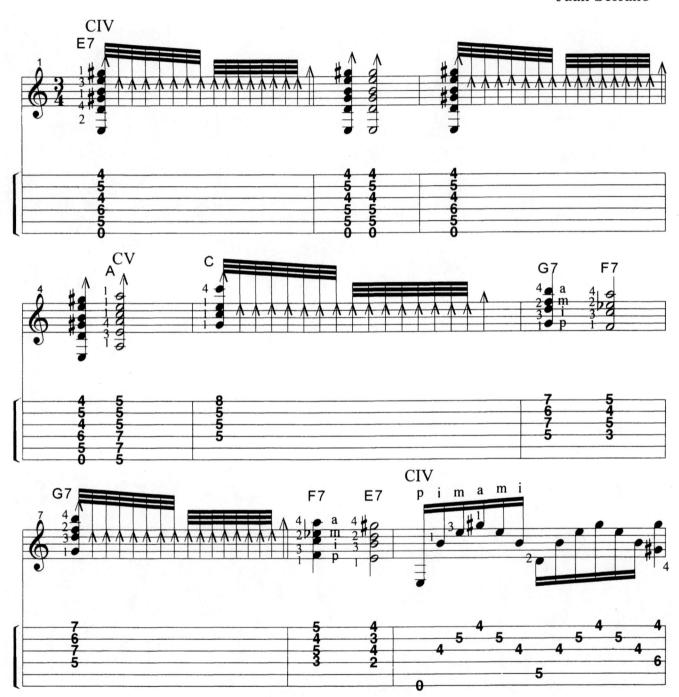

175

179

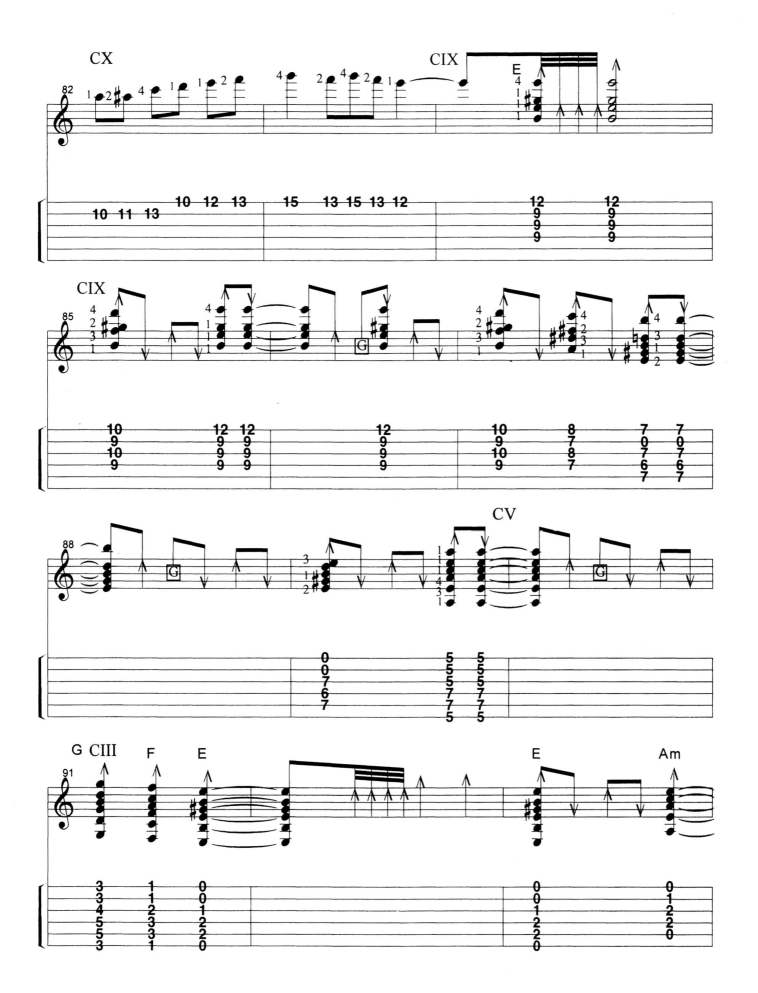

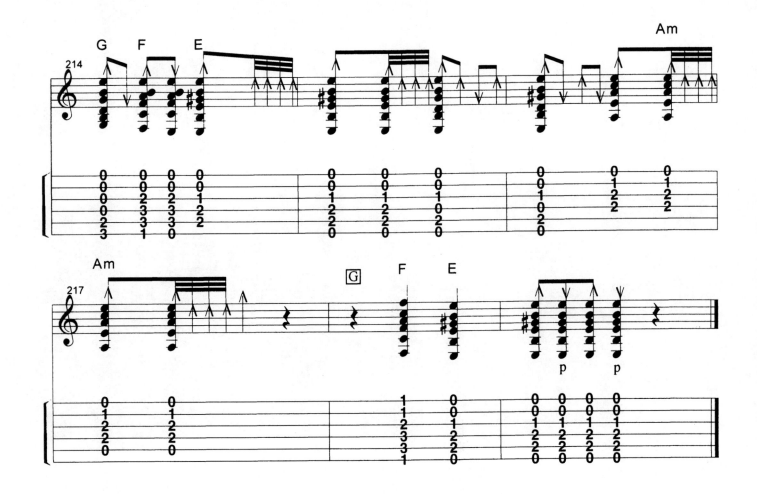

TARIFA

(Alegrias por medio—Derived from Soleares)

Juan Serrano

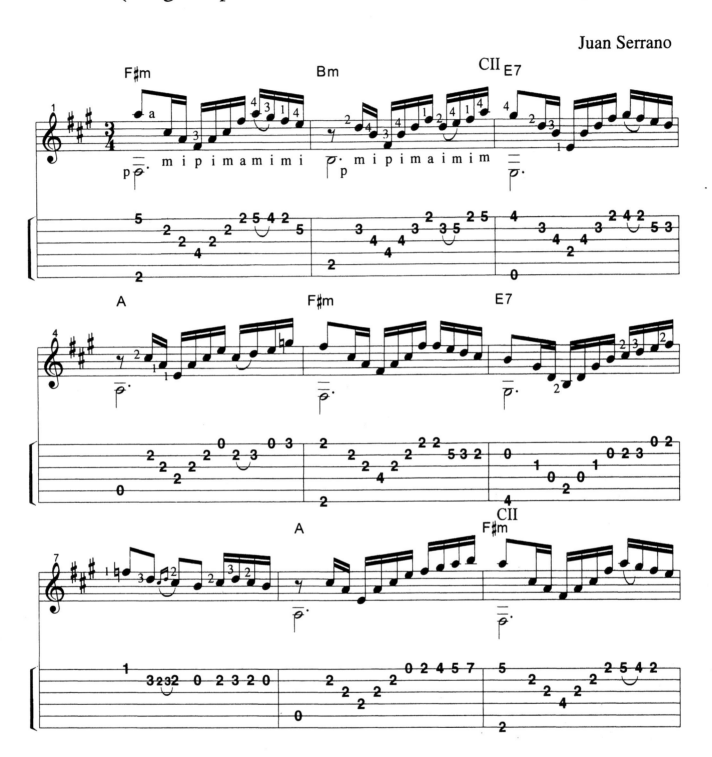

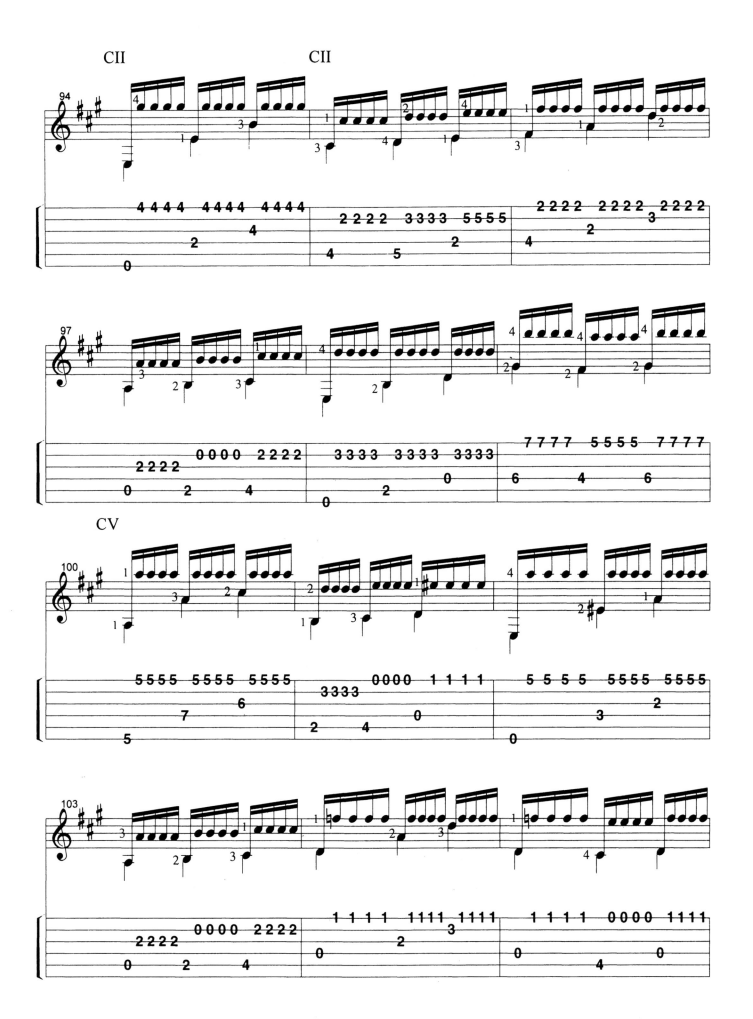

203

208

209

212

215

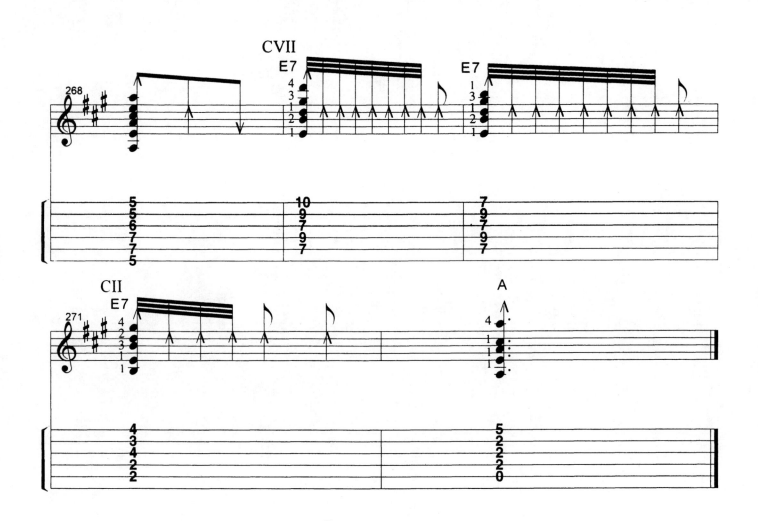

AMIGO MARIANO

(Colombianas—Derived from Tangos)

A Mariano Cordoba

Juan Serrano